LEARN COMPUTING

Fact Factory

Anne Rooney

QEB Publishing

Published in the United States by
QEB Publishing
23062 La Cadena Drive
Laguna Hills
Irvine
CA 92653

Library of Congress Catalog Control Number: 2004101528

ISBN 1-59566-042-9

Written by Anne Rooney
Consultant: Philip Stubbs
Designed by Jacqueline Palmer
Editor: Anna Claybourne
Illustrator: John Haslam
Photographer: Ray Moller
Models supplied by Scallywags

Creative Director: Louise Morley
Editorial Manager: Jean Coppendale

Printed and bound in China

The words in **bold** are
explained in the Glossary
on page 31.

Contents

Do you know what goes on in your brain? It's a huge information factory. Throughout your life you'll use it to learn lots of facts, make connections between them and store the ones you need to remember.

Un, deux, trois...

Yum yum! Baked beans for supper.

Tigers love swimming.

Brains and computers

You can store a huge amount of information in your brain —and there's so much you can do with it.

However, no one can remember everything they've ever learned, and we soon forget information we don't use very often. That's where a computer can help.

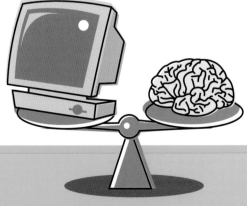

Full of facts

A computer system for storing, comparing, and sorting facts is called a database. A database can be very small and keep a specific set of facts, such as the heights of all the children in a class, or it can be very large and store huge amounts of information, such as details of every movie ever made.

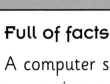

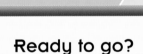

Ready to go?

In this book you'll find out how to use databases to find, use, and store information in lots of different ways. You'll make databases of your own to work with information you've gathered, and you'll use the Internet to collect even more useful facts.

Usually, a database groups together information that's related in some way. For example, it could store information about the members of a club or the things for sale in a supermarket.

Everyday databases

You could make a database of all your CDs, listing the artists, songs, and dates when each CD was released. Your school has a database of information about all the pupils. It has details like your name, address, and date of birth. If you belong to a fan club or library, or subscribe to a magazine, the organization probably has a database of all of its members, too.

There are databases all around us in our daily lives. If you use an encyclopedia on CD-ROM, that's a database. And if you buy things in a store and use a store card, the outlet's database keeps a record of what items you've bought.

GAME ZONE
Customer Club

Drew McCaskey
15745 82362 77854

Ultramarine Screen   Attack of the Zykorgs

Feb 22   8:30 $7.00

Fact-finding

Storing lots of information is all very good, but unless you can find the facts you want easily, it's not a very useful.

Imagine a big book of facts without an index. You know there's lots of information in there, but how are you going to find out what you need to know? Without an index, you'd just have to read through each page one by one. It would take a long time. Encyclopedias and phone books are arranged in alphabetical order.

Databases, too, need ways of helping you find information. Unlike a book, a database can change the order it shows you information. For example, you could look at a list of kings and queens in alphabetical or chronological order.

Paper or computer?

In all your work, it's important to think about whether you really need to use the computer, or whether there is a better way. In the case of working with facts and figures, a database on the computer is often the best method.

Basketball scores
Ty "Springer" Daniels 18 points
Zeb Watson 8 points
"Tall Paul" McCoy 1 points

Sport heroes

Imagine that you want to keep a list of the top players in a particular sport, and how many points or goals each one has scored. As more games are played, you add more details.

If you kept your notes on paper, you'd have to decide how to list the players—by team or alphabetically by name. You'd also need to add up the scores for each player. This would change each week, so you'd have to figure them out all over again.

If you kept your list on your computer, it could add up all the points for you, and tell you who had the best score so far every week.

This week's results...

You could use your sports data to make a set of collector's cards—one for each player.

How computers help

Keeping a database on a computer helps in several different ways:

- The computer can automatically compare facts or do calculations for you. On paper, you'd have to look through all of them and do the math yourself.

- You can easily sort information into any order, almost instantly. If you keep a list on paper, it takes some time to re-order your facts.

- You can print out your information any time you add new facts. On paper, you'd have to copy it all out again each time.

- A computer can find information very quickly, but on paper you have to read through the whole thing to find what you want.

Sometimes, though, a paper list may be better. You can carry it around easily with you, use it when you can't get to the computer, and add your own pictures or stickers.

Build your own database

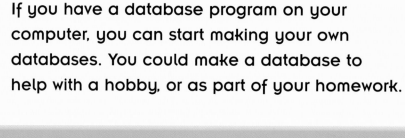

If you have a database program on your computer, you can start making your own databases. You could make a database to help with a hobby, or as part of your homework.

Think first

Before you start making your database, think about what information you want to put in it. You might have the information at hand, or you might have to collect facts for your database.

Doing a survey

One way to get information is to do a survey. You can draw up a list of questions on paper. If there are only a few possible answers to a question, use multiple choice questions with checkboxes for different options.

Survey questions

Make sure you ask relevant questions. For example, if you're finding out about cool places to visit, it's not relevant to ask people what their favorite color is.

Make your questions as useful as possible. Ask for their date of birth, not their age. Ages change every year, but a database can work out ages from dates of birth.

Date of birth
May 25,1994
age 10

Date of birth
July 19, 1982
age 22

Date of birth
April 30,1947
age 57

Question time

Imagine that you wanted to make a database of fun things to do in your town. You'd decide on the best questions, then make them into a data-collection sheet.

Cool things to do in our town

Please fill in details of your favorite place to go.

What is it called? _____

What type of place is it? (check one)

☐ Leisure center
☐ Movie theater
☐ Outdoor place (park, zoo, etc.)
☐ Bookstore/Library
☐ Other

What can you do there? _____

How much does it cost? (per hour/session) _____

What's the phone number? _____

Does it have a web address? _____

Thank you for taking part

Put it to the test

Next, decide who to include in your survey. Is your database only for young people, or should you ask people of all ages? Think about all the answers you might get and see if any of your questions could be better. For example, people might just answer "yes" to the last question—so you could change it to "What is the web address?"

Starting your database

After you've collected all the information you need, you can start to build your customized database.

Records and fields

A database divides information up into useful categories.

Each item for which you have information has its own **record**. In a database of cars, there'd be one record for each car.

Each fact in a record goes in a space called a **field**. In your car database, each record might have fields for the make, model, and engine size of the car.

If you made a database of horses at a stable, you'd have a record for each horse, with fields for the name, date of birth (D.O.B.), height, and color of the horse.

DO IT!

Using your database software, start a new database. The first thing to do is set up the types of fields that will be used in each record and give each field a name, such as "Date of birth" or "Phone number."

You'll need to choose the type of field—for example, numbers, text, or dates.

Name: Tora
D.O.B: 21.12.99
Height: 15 hands
Color: brown

Putting in your information

You put information into your database by typing in the fields on each record.

You need to make a new record for each item you have information about.

TAKE CARE

Check the information is correct before you enter it, and copy it into the computer carefully. The computer can't correct mistakes for you and you'll get the wrong answers out of the database if you put the wrong information in. When you've finished, print everything out and check it.

Cool places

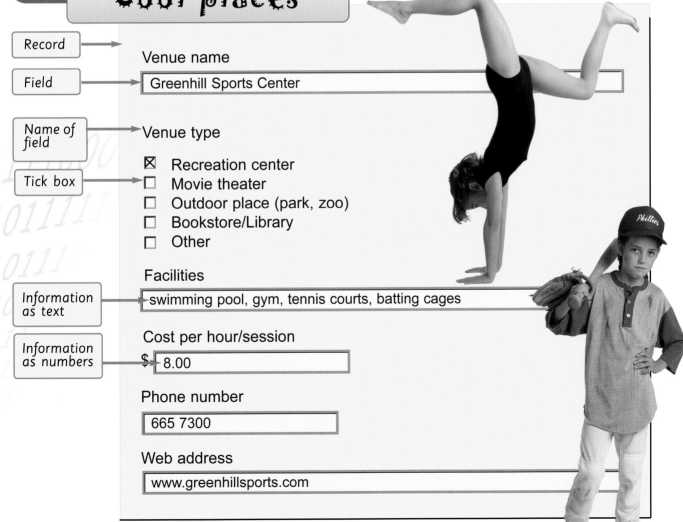

Record →	**Venue name**
Field →	Greenhill Sports Center
Name of field →	**Venue type**
Tick box →	☒ Recreation center
	☐ Movie theater
	☐ Outdoor place (park, zoo)
	☐ Bookstore/Library
	☐ Other
	Facilities
Information as text →	swimming pool, gym, tennis courts, batting cages
	Cost per hour/session
Information as numbers →	$ 8.00
	Phone number
	665 7300
	Web address
	www.greenhillsports.com

Making it work

After you've put all your information into your database, you can make lists, graphs, or charts from it.

Putting things in order

You can look at the information in your database in different ways by asking the database to put the records in order for you. This is called **sorting** the database.

For example, you might want your "Cool places" database to show you a list of places in order of price, with the cheapest first. To do this, you'd need to:

• Choose the field you want to see information about—in this case, it's the "Cost" field.

• Tell the computer how to sort the information. To see the cheapest prices first, tell the computer to list the entries in order of cost.

 DO IT!

In your database program, the option to sort your database will probably be called "Sort" or "Reorder." You should be able to choose ascending order (going up, for example, from A–Z or from 1–9) or descending order (going down, from Z–A or 9–1).

You can print out a list of the information in the order you've chosen.

Fantasy Arcade $4.00

Movieland $7.50

Greenhill Sports $8.00

Camden Zoo $10.00

Aquarium $12.00

Graphs and charts

Most databases will let you make a graph, using the information stored in them. It's usually easier to see facts by looking at a graph than by reading numbers.

Imagine that you had a database on people's pets. You could get the database to draw a graph to show how many children in your class had each type of pet.

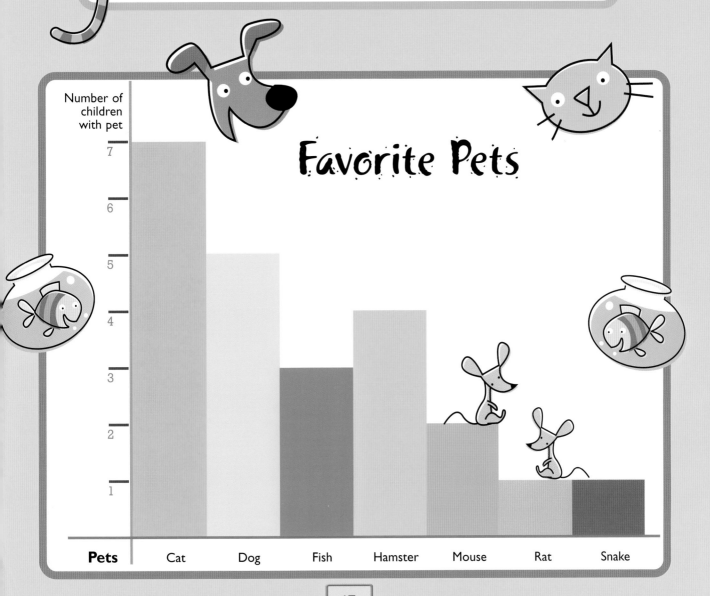

Favorite Pets

Number of children with pet

7
6
5
4
3
2
1

Pets | Cat | Dog | Fish | Hamster | Mouse | Rat | Snake

Looking up facts

Sometimes you will want to find particular items in a database. You'll need to tell the database what you're looking for and ask it to find anything that matches.

Ask the database

Suppose you want to use your "Cool places" database to find all the Recreation centers, or all the movie theaters. You find them by asking the database a question called a **query**, or by setting a **filter**.

To do this, you usually have to fill in a form on screen showing what you want to find. The computer will look for things in the fields you fill in. It will ignore any fields you leave blank.

For example, you could look for movies like this:

Venue name

[   ]

Venue type

☐ Recreation centers
☒ Movie theater
☐ Outdoor place (park, zoo, etc.)
☐ Bookstore/Library
☐ Other

Facilities

[   ]

Cost per hour/session

$ [   ]

Phone number

[   ]

Web address

[   ]

Finding out more

What if you want to find something specific—such as all movie theaters that cost less than $10 a ticket?

For things like this, you can use special symbols, called **operators**, to find numbers in a particular range.

This search would find cinemas that cost less than $10

Operators include:

= means equals
Cost=$10
means "find prices that are exactly $10"

> means more than
Cost>$10
means "find prices over $10"

< means less than
Cost<$10
means "find prices under $10"

Venue name

Venue type

☐ Recreation centers
☒ Movie theater
☐ Outdoor place (park, zoo, etc.)
☐ Bookstore/Library
☐ Other

Facilities

Cost per hour/session

$ <10

Phone number

Web address

Make it match

In some databases, you search for results by entering a whole phrase, such as "**Cost<$10**," into a search box. Make sure you always use the same words the database uses. For example, if a field is named "**Cost**," you must use the word "**Cost**," not a different word like "**Price**," because the computer won't recognize it.

Does not compute...!

The world's biggest database

The biggest database in the world is the World Wide Web. Everything you want to know is probably out there somewhere!

Get started

To use the World Wide Web, you need to make sure your computer is connected to the **Internet**, and start up a **web browser**, such as Internet Explorer or Netscape. Ask for help if you're not sure how to do this.

Starting from home

The page your web browser shows when it starts up is called your home page. You can always get back to it by clicking the Home button in your browser.

Moving around

If you know which web page you want to look at, type in its web address accurately, and then press the Enter or Return key.

Web links

When you get to the page you want, there could be links to other useful information. A link is usually underlined and shown in a different color, like this: <u>Great white shark</u>.

Going back

If you end up somewhere you don't want to be, or see something you're not comfortable with, click on the Back button to go back a page, or on the Home button to start again.

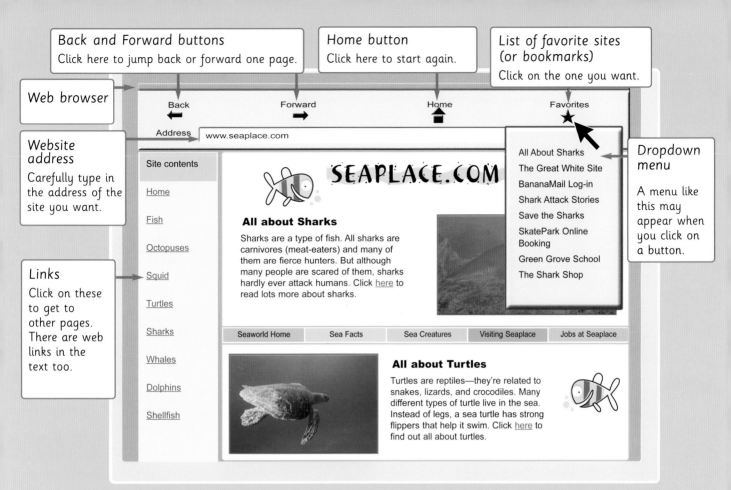

Back and Forward buttons
Click here to jump back or forward one page.

Home button
Click here to start again.

List of favorite sites (or bookmarks)
Click on the one you want.

Web browser

Website address
Carefully type in the address of the site you want.

Links
Click on these to get to other pages. There are web links in the text too.

Dropdown menu
A menu like this may appear when you click on a button.

Back   Forward   Home   Favorites

Address www.seaplace.com

All About Sharks
The Great White Site
BananaMail Log-in
Shark Attack Stories
Save the Sharks
SkatePark Online Booking
Green Grove School
The Shark Shop

SEAPLACE.COM

Site contents

Home

Fish

Octopuses

Squid

Turtles

Sharks

Whales

Dolphins

Shellfish

All about Sharks

Sharks are a type of fish. All sharks are carnivores (meat-eaters) and many of them are fierce hunters. But although many people are scared of them, sharks hardly ever attack humans. Click here to read lots more about sharks.

Seaworld Home | Sea Facts | Sea Creatures | Visiting Seaplace | Jobs at Seaplace

All about Turtles

Turtles are reptiles—they're related to snakes, lizards, and crocodiles. Many different types of turtle live in the sea. Instead of legs, a sea turtle has strong flippers that help it swim. Click here to find out all about turtles.

Best places

If you find a web page you like, and you think you might want to use it again, you can add it to a list of your favorite sites. If you're using Internet Explorer, these are called **Favorites**, and if you're using Netscape, they're called **Bookmarks**.

Make sure you have at least one really good, general homework site in your Favorites.

DO IT!

Open the Bookmarks or Favorites menu in your browser, and click on "Add" to add the page to your list. Remember what the page is called in the list, so that you can find it again later.

When you want to go back to it again, open the menu. Then click on the name of the page you want to go back to.

Finding what you want

There are two ways of finding what you want on the Internet. You can do a search, or you can use a contents list or directory, which lets you choose from different categories of information.

Working with directories

A **directory page** lists categories of information, such as "news," "sport," "homework help," and "entertainment." When you click on one, a list for that topic appears for you to choose again. Eventually, you should locate the information you want.

A directory is good if you know roughly what you want to find. If you want to read the latest news, or see which movies are just coming out, a directory can help.

DO IT!

Try these directory pages:

www.yahooligans.com
www.kidgrid.com
http://directory.google.com
(click on "Kids and Teens")

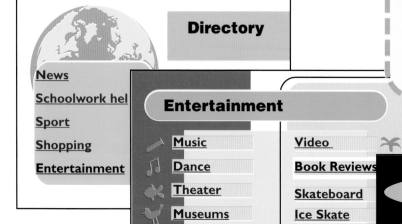

Directory

News
Schoolwork hel
Sport
Shopping
Entertainment

Entertainment

Music
Dance
Theater
Museums
Art

Video
Book Reviews
Skateboard
Ice Skate
Drama

Latest Movies

Attack of the Zykorgs
The Magic Skateboard
Beowulf

Searching the Internet

To find precise information, say a cake recipe, a search is better.

You search the Internet using a special kind of web page called a search page or **search engine**.

You'll need to type in the words you're looking for (called **keywords**), and click a button to start the search. The search engine will list pages that contain your keywords.

How to search

To search for a single word, type it and click the button:

| chocolate | **Search** |

To search for a phrase, put it in quotation marks:

| "chocolate brownies" | **Search** |

To search for several words or phrases, just put them all in:

| "chocolate brownies" recipes | **Search** |

or put "**+**" or "**AND**" between them:

| "chocolate brownies" + recipes | **Search** |

 DO IT!

Try these search pages:

www.google.com
www.yahoo.com
www.alltheweb.com
www.altavista.com

Choosing the best keywords takes practice. Don't search for "how to make chocolate brownies" because unless a web page has that exact phrase in it, you won't find anything. But don't be too vague, either. If you just put "recipes," you'd find thousands of pages and it would take you ages to track down brownies!

Checking your facts

Whether you've found information from your own database, from a **CD-ROM** or from the Internet, you need to have a good look at it and decide whether it's what you need.

Asking questions

Whatever you're going to do with the information you've found, you'll need to check that it's:

• Accurate • Reliable• Relevant

Make sure you think about all these things before you use the information you've found.

Accuracy

You can probably trust information you get from an encyclopedia or a CD-ROM to be accurate.

If it's from your own database, it will be right as long as you put in the right information and asked the right questions—so check! Think about the answers you'd expect to get, and if they're very different, check your work again.

• Reliable
–do you trust the place you got it from?

• Accurate
–is it right?

• Relevant
–is it suitable for what you want to use it for?

Reliability

If the information is from the Internet, is it from a website you can trust? Anyone can put up web pages and no one checks that they're accurate or true.

The information on websites can be biased, too. This means that the people who put up the website want you to think in a particular way.

Relevance

You could find some very interesting information, but if it isn't anything to do with the subject you're working on, it's not relevant—so leave it out!

I can trust this Encarta CD-ROM.

No

No to pollution

This protest site "Fight Pollution" may be biased ... But "The SciTech Museum Kid's Page—Pollution" looks good!

That's a cool pic of Dolly the cloned sheep! But I can't really put that in because it's not about pollution...

Think about what might happen if the answers you've got are wrong. It could make a big difference—if you typed in a recipe incorrectly, it could taste disgusting or even make you sick!

Sharing information

Storing lots of information is only the start. You need to do things with it—like presenting it in a way other people can understand, or printing it out to use later.

Database reports

If you're working with a database of your own, you can print out **reports** which show some or all of the information it stores.

Chocolate recipes

Recipe	Time it takes to make
Chocolate sauce	5 mins
Choc crispies	10 mins
Choco-cherry cookies	15 mins
Choc'n'flake cake	1 hour
Chocolate ice cream	6 hours

Before printing out your report, you may be able to choose different text styles and arrangements to make it look better.

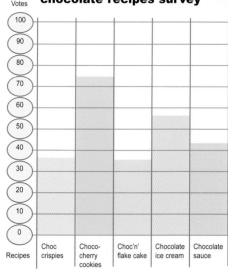

TOP TEN chocolate recipes survey

Votes: 100, 90, 80, 70, 60, 50, 40, 30, 20, 10, 0

Recipes: Choc crispies, Choco-cherry cookies, Choc'n' flake cake, Chocolate ice cream, Chocolate sauce

Internet Information

If you're working with information from the Internet —or from another large database such as a CD-ROM —you'll need to copy, save, or print the information you've found so you can use it for your projects.

You can:

• Print a page out, so you can show it to other people or look at it later.

• Save the page on your computer so that you can look at it without having to connect to the Internet or load the CD.

• Copy words and pictures from a page to put into your own work.

 ## DO IT!

To copy information from the Internet, use the mouse to select the words or pictures you want. Choose "Copy" from the menus at the top of the browser window. Then open a document of your own, and use the "Paste" option to stick in the info you've copied.

Don't steal!

Words and pictures on the Internet are someone else's work, and the law protects other people's work. It's OK to use a bit in something that's just for you, but you can't make lots of copies or include it in a book or a website without getting permission.

When you copy something from the Internet to use in your projects, always add a note of the web address where you found it. This will make it easy to check it again later, and will show you're not pretending it's your own work.

More projects to try

Now you know the score, it's time to try it all out for yourself. Here are some suggestions for projects—but, of course, you can change them to make them fit in with your own interests!

Music poster

Use the Internet to search for pictures of your favorite music group and information about them. Copy some of the stuff you find into a document of your own to make a poster or leaflet about them. You don't have to use the computer to make your poster. Instead, you could print out the words and pictures you find, and cut up the pages so that you can glue the best pieces onto posterboard to make a collage.

Pet-sitting project

Need to earn some extra allowance money? You could start a pet-sitting service—or just make a database of your friends' pets for fun.

If you really want to take care of pets, check with a grown-up first.

Pet database

Make a database for your pet-sitting service. You'll need a record for each pet. Decide what fields you need to put on each record.

It's a good idea to list different types of animals and check the right one on each record. Then you can find all the cats or all the mice with a simple search.

PET SITTING

Animal's name _____

Animal's age _____

Owner's name _____

Owner's phone number _____

Type of animal:

- ☐ Dog
- ☐ Cat
- ☐ Mouse
- ☐ Hamster
- ☐ Snake

Ask around

Carry out a survey to find out what kind of pets your friends have. Carefully copy the information into your database. Check the information you've added and try some searches and reports. Could you make the database better? Improve it and try it out again.

Secret spy club

Start a secret spy club with some friends, and keep all your spy details on a secret database. You'll need a record for each member. Decide on the fields you'll need for their details.

You could use your database to print out spy ID papers or membership cards for everyone.

Your database program may also let you include pictures, so you can add a photo of each spy and even their fingerprints, copied in with a **scanner**.

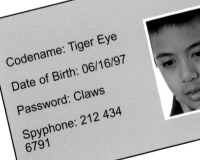

Codename: Tiger Eye

Date of Birth: 06/16/97

Password: Claws

Spyphone: 212 434 6791

TOP SECRET

Agent's name

Jimmy

Password

Claws

Codename

Tiger Eye

Date of birth

06/16/97

Spyphone

212 434 6791

Description

3 ft 5in tall; short black hair; brown eyes

Special skills

Judo black belt; Skateboard whizz kid

Details of missions

Spying on Shady Street. Inventing new codes.

Monsters!

Make a database of information about your favorite monsters— they could be dinosaurs, deep sea fish, monsters from movies or books, or monsters from myths and legends.

Collect all the information you can by searching the Internet, and then build a database with a record for each monster. Decide on all the different fields you will need on each record.

Here are some ideas for fields:

How big is each monster?

What does it eat?

What does it look like?

Where does it live?

You can also include a field for the addresses of the web pages where you found out about each monster.

Monster File........3

Monster name

Gorgon

Monster File........2

Monster name

Basilisk

Monster File........1

Monster name

Cyclops

Description

Hideously ugly, with messy hair and one eye in the middle of the forehead

Diet

Cheese, with occasional raw humans

Home

Caves on an island in the Mediterranean Sea

Info from:

www.mythsandlegends.com

Grown-up zone

Fact Factory

This book will help a child to:

- Use a database to record the results of a science experiment or class survey, then present or process the data to show trends or calculate values

- Use the Internet to search for information needed for a topic or theme in English or history

- Use an existing database, such as a CD-ROM, to search for facts needed for a geography report

Fact Factory helps children practice essential skills and tools they will need throughout their education, putting them on the road to good working habits and familiarity and ease with computer technology.

Work with your children to enable them to incorporate planning, drafting, checking, and reviewing their work in all projects they do and as a matter of habit. Ask them to discuss how their work could be improved, whether computer methods are the best choice for the job at hand, and how computer methods compare with manual methods. They should look at ways of combining information technology and manual methods of working.

Curriculum resources online

Education World: Technology in the Classroom:

www.educationworld.com/a_tech/

Educational Technology in the Federal Resources for Educational Excellence collection:

wdcrobcolp01.ed.gov/cfapps/free/displaysubject.cfm?sid=2

International Society for Technology in Education:

www.iste.org/resources/

Resources

It's important to make sure that children use the World Wide Web safely. The following sites give advice on how you can protect your children when they work online and how to help them use the Internet sensibly.

www.safekids.com

www.thinkuknow.co.uk

www.yahooligans.com/parents/

www.getnetwise.org

Glossary

Bookmark

Saved reference to a web page you want to use again.

Directory page

Web page that lists different topics to help you find a particular subject.

Favorite

Saved reference to a web page you want to use again.

Field

Space on a database record for a single item of information about something.

Filter

Way of finding records in a database that match specific requirements.

Internet

Network of computers connected together around the world so that they can share information.

Keyword

Word used to search the World Wide Web or another database.

Operator

Special word or symbol used to help you find information in a database.

Query

Question that you ask in order to find information.

Record

All the information about one particular item in a database.

Report

Printout or screen display of information found in a database.

Scanner

Device for copying pictures from paper into the computer.

Search engine

Web page used to search the World Wide Web.

Sort

Used to put information from a database into a particular order.

Web browser

Computer program for looking at and moving between web pages.

Index